Around Town

Shapes

W9-AXM-672

James D. Anderson

Consultants

Chandra C. Prough, M.S.Ed.
National Board Certified
Newport-Mesa
  Unified School District

Jodene Smith, M.A.
ABC Unified School District

Publishing Credits

Dona Herweck Rice, *Editor-in-Chief*
Lee Aucoin, *Creative Director*
Chris McIntyre, M.A.Ed., *Editorial Director*
James Anderson, M.S.Ed., *Editor*
Aubrie Nielsen, M.S.Ed., *Associate Education Editor*
Neri Garcia, *Senior Designer*
Stephanie Reid, *Photo Editor*
Rachelle Cracchiolo, M.S.Ed., *Publisher*

Image Credits

p.5 Juri Bizgajmer/Dreamstime; p.8 Natalia Bratslavsky/Dreamstime; p.12 Photolibrary; p.28 Michael DeLeon/iStockphoto; All other images: Shutterstock

Teacher Created Materials

5301 Oceanus Drive
Huntington Beach, CA 92649-1030
http://www.tcmpub.com
ISBN 978-1-4333-3438-2
© 2012 Teacher Created Materials, Inc.
BP 5028

Table of Contents

Shapes are all around.

Find the shapes around town.

This is a **rectangle**.

A rectangle has four sides.

A rectangle has four **corners**.

Find the rectangles.

This is a **square**.

A square has four **equal** sides.

A square has four corners.

Find the squares.

This is a **triangle**.

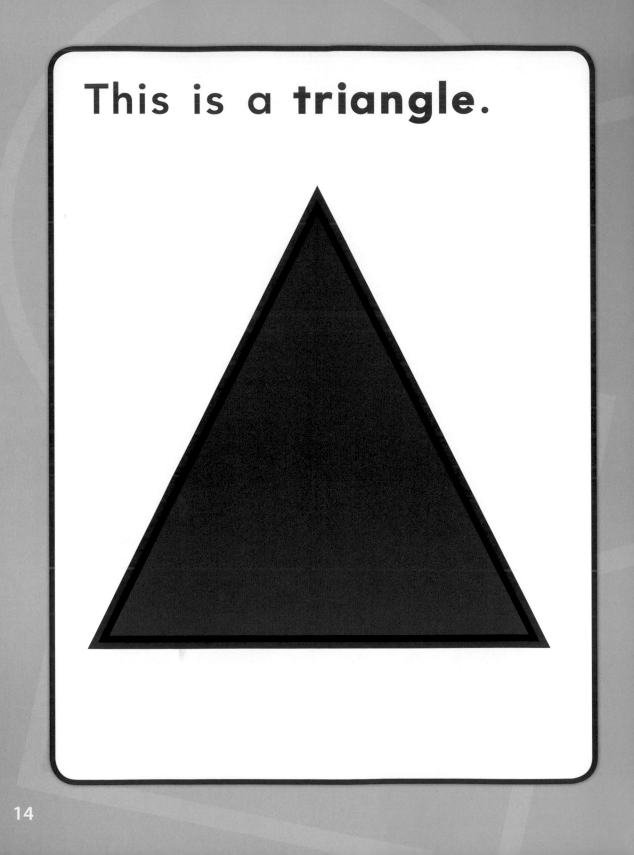

A triangle has three sides.

SCHOOL

A triangle has three corners.

Find the triangles.

This is a **circle**.

A circle is round.

A circle has no corners.

Find the circles.

Find the shapes around town!

Can you find the circles?

Can you find the squares?

Can you find the rectangles?

Can you find the triangles?

How can you use craft sticks to make shapes?

Materials
- ✓ craft sticks
- ✓ glue

1 Make a rectangle.

2 Make a square.

3 Make a triangle.

4 Can you make a circle?

Glossary

circle—a round shape with no sides and no corners

corners—the points where two sides meet

equal—the same length

rectangle—a shape with four sides and four corners

square—a shape with four equal sides and four corners

triangle—a shape with three sides and three corners

You Try It!

Pages 24–25:

circles:

squares:

Pages 26–27:

rectangles:

triangles:

Solve the Problem

Students should create rectangles, squares, and triangles out of craft sticks. Students should recognize that a circle cannot be made out of sticks because it has no straight sides and no corners.